BREAK-UP

TO

BREAKTHROUGH

Dalia Smith

Copyright

Preface

Loss

noun \'l's\

Simple Definition of LOSS

> A: failure to keep or to continue to have something
>
> B: the experience of having something taken from you or destroyed

Full Definition of LOSS

> 1: destruction, ruin
>
> 2a: the act of losing possession: deprivation <loss of sight> b: the harm or privation resulting from loss or separation c: an instance of losing

Above is Webster's dictionary definition of the word "loss." If you are reading this, you may have just gone through a loss. In this definition of loss, we are not talking about losing your keys or a death in the family. We're speaking of that loss that so many of us go through too many times in a lifetime, too many times to count, a break-up. The simple definition, both A and B seems to word it perfectly: "failure to keep or to continue to have something"; "the experience of having something taken from you or destroyed." It does feel like you failed in keeping something. Regardless of your gender, race, or the reason why the break-up occurred, you feel like you failed in keeping something. Something that you worked at, something that you invested in heavily.

On the other hand, it also feels like you had something taken from you and destroyed; the relationship that you procured, that you nurtured, that you spent time out of every hour in every day in order to make sure that it would be great. You spent your time to make sure that this relationship would be the last relationship that you ever had. It was destroyed. It was taken from you; it almost feels like a robbery to an extent. It feels like that person that you once knew was essentially hijacked for one day, putting an end to everything the two of you built. But which is it? Were they hijacked for that one day, becoming someone else, someone that you didn't even know? Or were they that person the entire length of the relationship? This person you just happened to find out their true self on that one day. The day that changed your life. The day that changed your relationship status. I don't mean on social media. We are talking about in real life. Now you may be like me where I don't care about what my relationship status says on Facebook, Twitter, Instagram or anywhere else. I don't need to change my status there. I do, however, need to do a swipe—a swipe of all the pictures on various social media pages. That's one of the worst parts; the part where you have to seemingly delete half of your pictures, half of your photographic life erased because of one person. You begin deleting photos of some of your favorite places because you no longer want to see them again.

This is where the simple definition impedes on the full definition. This happens when the end of the relationship encroaches into your full life, when other people have to be notified in an act of recourse. Most of us don't want, nor need, to place an ad out to our friends and family to say "HEY, I'M NO LONGER IN A RELATIONSHIP!" However, day to day conversations will almost always lead to that. A general conversation seems to lead to "Hey, how's... (insert name that we wish to no longer hear here)?" That is when Webster's full definition kicks in. 1: destruction, ruin. Now all the conversations you now go through must have a disclaimer; a section in that conversation where you have to explain to your closest friends and family what happened and why.

To say the least, we've all been through these moments. We deal with them in different ways. Some of us sit around the house analyzing what went wrong, what we could've done so that it didn't end. Some of us just sit around the house, endlessly. Then some of us go to replacement mode, like when you go out as often as humanly possible in order to find someone new or just to find someone so that we don't have to think about the person we are getting over. So, how do you get over it? More importantly, how do you overcome? *Break-up to Breakthrough* is my story of how I did just that. My break-up, on the surface, seems like any other breakup that any woman has been through, that's until you peel back the layers and you see exactly what happened and why. Lastly, *Break-up to Breakthrough* leads to an incredible revelation—this is the most important part. Relationships serve as lessons—these lessons are up to us to figure out. The break-up doesn't come with a note or a warning that states what you should learn. But if we truly pay attention, if we truly keep our eyes open, we will see that there is a hidden lesson in everything. Each relationship and each breakup shares a valuable lesson. This lesson is up to us to decode. *Break-up to Breakthrough* is about me decoding my life-changing lesson.

This is for every woman who has had her heart broken. Every woman who has thought she was not good enough.

Table of Contents

- Developing Healthy Relationship Skills: Complementing Each Other, Disagreeing Productively, Fighting Fair, Listening and Being Heard
- Don't Be a Doormat

- The Most Important Relationship You Will Ever Have is with Yourself
- You Become Irresistible to Others When You Accept Yourself Completely
- Stop Waiting: Enjoy the "Now Moments"
- The Importance of Self-Care: Be Your Highest Priority
- Who Cares What the World Thinks?
- Commit to Loving and Respecting Yourself

- Transitioning: Accept The Past And Move On
- The Beauty of Being Single
- Develop Deeper Self-Respect and Self-Acceptance
- Feel More Calm and Resilient within Yourself
- Is Low Self-Worth Keeping You From Moving On?

Acknowledgements

I would like to express my sincere gratitude to my family and friends for their love, guidance, and support throughout the course of my healing. Thank you for weathering the storm with me.

Disclaimer

I have tried to recreate events, locales, and conversations from my memories of them. In order to maintain their anonymity in some instances, I have changed the names of individuals and places, I may have changed some identifying characteristics and details such as physical properties, occupations and places of residence.

Introduction

*T*his book is a very profound and intimate look at my broken engagement and journey toward everlasting self-love. Personal and deep, I am going to be real with you about my own heartbreak and healing. Perhaps you're asking why I want to share my private life with the entire world. After all, these were some of the most intimate details of my life and heart, and most people tend to be a little more discrete when it comes to heartbreak and infidelity.

But I want you to know that you're not alone. If you're going through something similar—heartbreak of any kind—my traumatic experience will feel like home to you, but not for long. I'm hoping to show you that it is possible to climb out of the darkness of depression and humiliation, just as I have. Also, in being open and honest, I began to experience true healing. I knew people would soon start talking and question what went wrong, so Break-up to Breakthrough

I reached out to my close friends and family and the more I spoke about it, the easier it became. Opening up also helped me realize that I had dodged a major bullet and had no reason to be embarrassed. I outsmarted a con artist, stood up for myself, and found an inner strength I did not know I had. I figured if I had the courage to share my story, I would be able to use my new life lessons to help other women gain the courage to escape unhealthy relationships.

During the course of my relationship and even after the end of my engagement, I had been saving every text message, photo, and email exchanged with my ex, wedding planner, and boss (to be brutally honest…I also needed the evidence in case I ended up going to court to get the wedding expenses reimbursed). Some of these will be shared in my book.

I've been through a lot. Some parts of my story I wouldn't wish on anyone else—ever. Yet, I wouldn't change my story for the world. I have no regrets. After surviving what I thought would kill me, I felt compelled to write this book and help others. Through my pain, perhaps I can help others experience beauty and joy again too.

This book is for any woman who has ever struggled with self-love, doubt, fear, insecurity, and a toxic relationship. If you, at this very moment, find yourself caught up in a struggle with self-love, this book was written for you.

I share how I went from break-up to breakthrough. And now it's your turn. If you give this book a chance and allow it to guide you, you can avoid making the exact mistakes I made. And you can experience a free and radiant life after heartache too!

SECTION 1
The Engagement Story

Chapter 1
Marriage Soon

"Everybody's looking for love, and you want to love somebody and be loved in return." —Jill Scott

It all began winter 2011. I remember the day so clearly. I was in my 2000 Ford Escort driving down the streets of Washington, DC, crying to some Mariah Carey love songs. Yeah—that happened. Not a proud moment. But unfortunately, that was just one of the many moments I'm not proud of. I was so hungry for love. Singlehood just wasn't for me. Dating just to date never appealed to me. I felt ready to settle down, be someone's wife, and start a family. But, I had no prospects. I decided at that moment I was going to join a dating site. I had tried other dating sites before, and after going on dates with many jerks and having many "hell dates," I decided enough was enough. I was ready for my happily ever after. No more being jerked around and patiently waiting for "Mr. Right." So, that evening, as I laid in bed getting ready to go to sleep, I created a profile on Match.com. Two weeks went by, and after maybe three or four unsuccessful dates, I came across Andrew's photo. I was instantly attracted. As I started reading his profile, I couldn't believe this guy was single. He seemed like such a catch. On paper, he was everything I could have hoped for and more. I can't recall who messaged whom first, but I believe I sent him a "wink" and he "winked" back and followed up with a message. Our first date was amazing. He took me to a very nice restaurant at the National Harbor. Honestly, at first, I was a bit skeptical I was almost in disbelief when he walked in the restaurant and approached me. He was at least 20lbs lighter than he looked in his profile photos. I wasn't as attracted to him. I thought to myself, "Well, this should be interesting." The date ended up lasting 8 hours. We talked and talked all night long. At the end of the night, he walked me back to my car, shook my hand, and said goodnight. I wasn't sure if I was going to hear from him again. I'd never had a man shake my hand before. If anything, I thought I would get a hug and maybe a kiss on the cheek. Two days later, I got a message from him on Match, telling me how he had a good time and that he hoped to see me again. I was ecstatic to know the feelings were mutual. Due to his crazy work schedule and frequent travels to New York, our second and third dates were pretty spaced apart, and we didn't talk that much in between. Things eventually fizzled out, but a few months later, he contacted me and we started talking again and eventually started dating again.

One night I went on Match to see if his profile was still up, and sure enough, it was. Not only did his profile exist, but the green icon was on showing that he was online at that very moment. I was infuriated. Although we had never had a discussion about it, I had cancelled my account as I just assumed that the feeling was mutual and that we were seeing each other exclusively.

We were supposed to have dinner that night, but I was so upset that I decided I was done with him and made plans to go out with some of my girlfriends instead. Andrew must have called me about 25 times that night and left numerous texts. I ignored them all. Instead, I went out to my favorite lounge downtown and danced the night away.

After a few drinks, I got a little weak and decided to finally respond. I told him that I clearly was not the woman for him and that I didn't want to see him anymore. He called me right away. I texted him telling him I was out and could not talk, but that I knew he still had a profile on Match. Of course he denied it. He insisted he had deactivated his account long ago and said he was going to call Match in the morning to file a report. I then unleashed everything I had ever held in. Everything that he did and did not do that upset me. I acknowledged the fact that he had had trust issues after having been supposedly betrayed in the past by different women but pointed out that I didn't, and wouldn't continue to prove to him that I was a good person and not like the others.

Finally, after a few more texts, he apologized for his behavior and told me he wanted me to be his girlfriend. I was overjoyed. That night I went to bed with the biggest smile on my face. The next day he had me come over, and we spent the entire day together. He brought up Match.com once again and said their customer representative department was closed but that he was going to contact them first thing Monday morning as their "screw up" could have potentially prevented us from being together. Apparently, he did speak to a Customer Representative at Match.com who apologized for everything.

From that very day, Andrew did a complete 360. He became everything I could have hoped for in a boyfriend and more. He was affectionate, romantic, supportive, etc. Every night when I said my prayers, I made sure to thank God for blessing me with such an amazing man. I had never felt so much love in my heart. And I just knew Andrew was the one I wanted to spend the rest of my life with.

At the end of our first summer together, Andrew brought up getting engaged. As excited as I was, I remember being a bit hesitant, and asking him if he didn't think it was too soon.

After all, we had only been "officially" together for a few months. He told me time meant nothing and that we had known each other long enough to know whether or not we wanted to get married to each other. I agreed. Time didn't mean a thing.

One night while we were sitting at the Cheesecake Factory waiting for our dinner to be served, Andrew decided to be silly and sent me a text message of a ring pop and said, "Will you marry me?" I was in a bad mood, so I just replied "No." He then sent me a photo of a ring that he had looked at in person at Helzberg Diamonds. My mouth dropped. The ring was absolutely gorgeous. He told me a few weeks later that he had made a deposit. I was so excited but asked him to wait until after I finished my graduate studies as I wanted to stay focused and not get off track. I knew if I got engaged I would be so excited and perhaps spend too much time on Pinterest instead of finishing my thesis. A few months went by, and still no ring. I was getting impatient and, quite honestly, I was pretty upset. After having seen the ring, you can only imagine how anxious I was to have that diamond on my finger.

Valentine's Day came and I was sure the proposal was going to happen that day. Wrong. Andrew gave me a small jewelry box with a pendant and earrings (which came from Helzberg). Upset is an understatement. I was furious. The following night, as I was standing at my bedroom dresser getting ready for bed, I heard Andrew say, "Hey babe." I turned around and saw him laying on the bed with an open jewelry box in hand. "Will you marry me?" he said. I couldn't believe it. My jaw dropped. I jumped on the bed and kissed him and said, "Yes!" I couldn't believe it. I was finally engaged. It was the best feeling in the world. Almost felt too good to be true. I couldn't believe we were finally engaged. After all the heartbreaks I had endured in the past, I had finally found my love, my soulmate, my best friend who I was going to spend the rest of my life with. I couldn't wait to get married.

After telling my family and close friends, I couldn't wait to make the announcement on Facebook. As I posted a photo of my ring with the caption "Can't wait to spend the rest of my life with my best friend" and changed my relationship status from "In a Relationship" to "Engaged" nervousness swept over me. While I can't exactly put it into words, deep down I had a feeling that I was going to regret my public announcement. Also, I can't tell you how disappointed I was about the marriage proposal. I had fantasized about that very moment for so long. I watched movies, looked up YouTube videos—you name it. Not gonna lie, I even practiced my reaction. C'mon, you ladies all know it has at least crossed your mind once—if not more. While I knew it most likely would not be any fairytale proposal ('cause let's face it, life is not like it is in the movies), I did think it would be special. I had somewhat high expectations. And I knew I was worthy of a special, romantic, thoughtful marriage proposal.

But, I was so happy to be off the market that I just let it go and focused on wedding planning. So, the planning began.

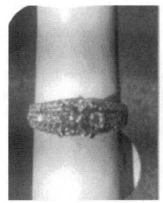

I joined "The Knot," created our wedding website, pinned away on Pinterest, researched wedding venues, photographers, etc. Finally, after deciding on the wedding venue, we chose to get married at the Marina del Rey in Bronx, NY on Thursday, April 24, 2014. I was over the moon. The place was absolutely gorgeous.

We later went on to hire a wedding coordinator, photographer/videographer, etc. My parents were living overseas at the time, and since I had to pre-order my dress a certain amount of time before the wedding, I had to go wedding dress shopping without my mother. I was devastated. I had always imagined my mother with me as I tried on wedding dresses, helping me pick out the "right one." The first time I went dress shopping was with my older sister in New York City.

After trying on several dresses, I left empty handed due to the prices being out of my budget. The second time was in Maryland with my cousin. I fell in love with a dress that day. Never in my life had I felt so beautiful. I looked at my reflection in the mirror and couldn't help but smile from ear to ear. "I'm going to be a bride," I thought to myself. After seeing the look on both my cousin's and the sales persons' faces, I decided the dress was "the one." I put the dress on hold and as I drove home that I day, I texted Andrew and told him the good news. He then responded by telling me he couldn't wait to see me in the dress.

The next several months got a bit complicated. Andrew was Roman Catholic, and although he and his family did not ever go to church, they were still very firm in their beliefs. This meant they expected a traditional church wedding with a priest and everything. Although I was born and raised Muslim, I never practiced and was never very religious. To be brutally honest, religion was never important to me. I always felt as though instead of uniting people, it caused a division and tension. Because religion was very important to Andrew, it became important to me. I not only agreed to raise our future children Catholic, but I also agreed to have a Confirmation, with the understanding that we would fully practice Catholicism, attend church as much as possible, and carry Catholic values into everyday life.

Fall 2013 came, and so did the U.S government shutdown. Besides being an owner of a chimney cleaning company, Andrew was also allegedly a supervisor for the FBI's "Anti-Terrorism Unit." When everything happened with the government operations and agencies, it was only natural that he had to take on special assignments given that we were residing in the Washington D.C area. For almost two months I hardly saw him. It was tough—for me that is. He was supposedly working all day on chimneys, and at night, stationed outside of government officials' homes for overnight shifts. A couple of months before, the pave diamonds on my engagement ring were falling out, and we had to turn in my ring to the jeweler twice for a long period to have it repaired. I was devastated. I went four months without a ring on my finger. When my parents moved back home from being overseas, they did not even get a chance to lay eyes on my ring.

It became so frustrating having to explain to them and everyone why I did not have my ring. Finally, after going back and forth with the jeweler, Andrew was able to get reimbursed for the ring, so we went to another jeweler to find a different one. I was so upset. I loved my ring. Not only was it absolutely gorgeous, but it was the ring that Andrew used to propose with me. It saddened me that I had to put any other ring on my finger. After shopping for what felt like forever to me, we finally found another. It was a few thousand dollars more than my original, but because Andrew felt bad about me having a naked finger for so long, he decided to splurge and get me it. Three weeks went by and the ring was not ready as expected. I grew more and more impatient. This was not what an engagement was supposed to be like. I was very upset. Andrew and I had quite a few arguments about it.

Finally, when the ring was ready, Andrew didn't pick it up right away. This just boggled my mind. Why on Earth would this not be on the top of his priority list when he knew how long I had gone without a ring? I was outraged and was willing to do anything and everything possible to get my ring. I even offered to pick it up. Andrew called me one afternoon and told me the jeweler informed him that there was an issue with the ring and it would be a longer wait. Between my ring and Andrew's absence, I nearly lost my mind. I hardly saw him and felt like he didn't make an effort to see me between jobs. I came down with a terrible cold one day and still went a week without seeing him. I called the jeweler to check up on the ring and was told that a purchase history under his name did not exist. Of course, I told them they were greatly mistaken and made sure they had the correct spelling of his last name. They checked again and told me that Andrew had called about the ring but they had no record of him ever purchasing it. I hung up and told Andrew what happened and he was outraged.

He insisted it was a mistake and said he would take care of it. Furious, I went ahead and wrote a very angry Yelp review hoping that would light a fire under their ass. Well, it worked. The owner called me within minutes to discuss the matter. He apologized for the confusion and informed me that he could not find

Andrew's name in his system and told me to have him call him. I hung up and told Andrew what happened. He was, of course, upset that I had posted a negative review and told me not to worry and that he would take care of it but was busy working. I was so upset that I told him to request a refund and get me a ring elsewhere. Andrew agreed.

A week or two later I got a text from Andrew telling me that his godmother had passed away and he had to go back home to New York City for the funeral. Of course, I assumed I was going to go with him. After all, I was his fiancée. His loss was my loss. Well, he made it clear he was going alone and would be back in a few days. I was very bothered about it and told him so. He told me that it would be awkward because I would not know many people there. So, I stayed back. A few hours after the funeral, I get a text message from Andrew telling me that he had learned that several of his family members had an issue with him being in an interracial relationship and were against us getting married. I was in complete shock. It got worse. He told me that his father admitted to never condoning our relationship and spoke up and said he would not attend our wedding. Also, two out of three of his brothers had supposedly made some racist comments about me, along with an uncle I had never even met before. Andrew said he wanted to marry me, but he knew I was emotional and that I could not tolerate his family possibly saying negative things about me in person even when he would defend me. He said if I thought I was strong enough to endure that for as long as it took, then he was willing to proceed with the wedding plans. He just didn't want me to be hurt and felt bad that his family was being this way.

To have these racist views appear out of nowhere by so many different people in Andrew's family, especially after we had been engaged for months and months (nine to be exact), was a complete shock. His father had always been more than welcoming. From the first time I ever visited Andrew's parent's home, I was told to make myself at home and help myself to anything and everything. I received random gifts, stayed the weekend on numerous occasions, and even went on vacation with the entire family.

I could have speculated about his family members and whether they were capable of changing; however, I realized that while change and transformation are possible, it was ultimately a major gamble. Was Andrew willing to stand up to any of his family members and command their respect toward me? If his family was determined to mistreat me, was he willing to cut them off? Was I willing to go through my life with no connection to his side of the family? Was I willing for my future children to have no relationship with certain members on his side of the family, if it came to that? Was I willing to endure gossip, awkward moments, tension, and hatred from his family? All these questions ran through my mind over and over. There was so much to decide, and I almost felt as though I had to rush and come to a decision as not only were there many financial obligations to figure out, but my life was on pause. If we were going to part ways, I wanted to start the healing process as I knew it would certainly take a long time to recover. I kept hoping and praying that things might change after a while and if anything, his family could at least be polite and cordial with me so that it would not be uncomfortable to be in the same room. I did fear though that a child would make things worse and that I would have to worry about remarks being said to and/or in front of our child.

I wasn't sure how strong Andrew's love for me was and if he was willing to work hard to stay together. He was constantly trying to please everyone and avoid fighting with his family. I had tried to explain to him that he can still get his point across without it being a huge argument. I had plenty of faith that our relationship could have worked out despite our cultural differences, but only if he was actually willing to do so. So many concerns. Crazy, huh? Well, there's more—a lot more.

When my Andrew returned from his trip, he told me he had to go out of town for work. I never had a chance to discuss matters in person. He told me he still wanted to find a solution to the whole family fiasco and if I thought of anything to let him know and we would meet in person to talk once he got back into town. The night came, but Andrew never showed up. I called and texted him several times—No response. I sent him one final text: "You're obviously not in this. There's something that has your attention, and it's not me. It's a shame that you aren't the person I fell in love with and put my trust in and called my best friend. I guess the only thing I can do is move on with my life." His response: "Got hit by a bus last night coming from airport in work car with partner. I'm OK but still at hospital. Ttyl. I'll send you your stuff and a check." I couldn't believe it. After a few more texts back and forth, and me demanding he man up and speak to me in person, he agreed to find time to meet with me.

One afternoon I decided to go to my parent's house to fill them in on everything. I tried to stay strong and pretend I was

1 3

fine, but I eventually broke down in tears and told them everything. To my disbelief, while they were upset and shocked, they actually had faith that Andrew's family would come around and told me I should meet with him and try to work things out. I was completely shocked. I sat there crying hysterically telling them all that was said about me and our relationship and they still supported our union. I couldn't believe it. That moment right there gave me hope. I contacted Andrew and told him about my conversation with my parents and told him if us being together is what he absolutely wants, we needed to meet up so we could talk. He told me he took another "assignment" out of town to clear his head for about four days but wanted to see me when he got back.

Chapter 2
Moment Of Truth

"A lie cannot live." —Martin Luther King Jr

*I*was so desperate to work things out and proceed with the wedding and marriage that I decided to reach out to a friend about what was going on as I knew she had initially had some family issues when she and her boyfriend first got together.

She is Caucasian and her father was not pleased that she was dating an African-American man and had made some very inappropriate comments about their child. This friend of mine had a feeling that Andrew was using race as an excuse and that it was much deeper than that. She believed Andrew was being a coward and was deliberately hiding behind texts and calls because he did not want to confront me and tell me the truth. She suspected he was cheating on me. So, she decided to do some investigating for me. Nothing came up. Curiosity got the best of me and so I decided to do a random search on Angie's list to look up his business. Honestly, I had no idea what I was looking for. As I skimmed his profile, I suddenly realized a different address was listed under his chimney business name. Andrew was a contractor, and I knew that the mailing address listed on the site had to be accurate as that is where the check were mailed to. I quickly typed the address on the "Notes" app on my iPhone. This address was exactly where we used to live except it was a different apartment number. It didn't make any sense. Although I had always told myself I would never be the girl who does a drive by, I knew I owed it to myself to at least check it out. At that point, I had absolutely nothing to lose. So I did just that.

As I walk up to the apartment building, thinking I'm wasting my time, I suddenly see Andrew's friend, James outside by the front door smoking a cigarette. He was a friend from New York City whom Andrew had claimed to no longer be speaking to due to a big fallout. We were both shocked to see each other. After exchanging an awkward "Hey," I ask James what he is doing there. He tells me he is visiting Andrew and that he is upstairs with his new fiancé. I ignore him and quickly walk back to my car, my hands trembling, and immediately begin texting Andrew. Not only did he lie to me and was not out of town for "business," but he had a secret home that I did not know about. A secret home while he was living with me in my condo while we were actively house hunting. In fact, we had recently placed an offer (so he told me) on a house we had fallen in love with a couple of weeks before.

I call Andrew, and James picks up the phone. James tells me Andrew is with a girl he met in Romania a few months back and that I could go and see for myself if I didn't believe him. I quickly turn my car around on the highway and speed my way back to his place. I angrily march on over to the apartment and start speaking to James who is back outside where I had just left him.

Andrew had previously told me he was keeping his things in storage since my condo is small and we were getting ready to move into the house we were about to close on. All lies. The front door is open and everything is decorated. Pictures hung up on the wall, dining area set up, etc. I glance down and notice a pair of women's shoes on the floor by the door. When I look back up, James is smiling at me. He tells me he had told Andrew that he had to tell me the truth, and that Andrew was a compulsive liar. He acknowledges the fact that I had never liked him, but tells me he has no reason to lie about anything.

I confirm the fact that I do not like him and inform him that this present issue was strictly between Andrew and me. James calls Andrew to come downstairs. Andrew yells back that he is on the phone with his mother. Finally, I run inside and go upstairs. He looks at me, both shocked and infuriated. I see a girl coming out of his bedroom standing behind him looking puzzled. And no, I don't say a word to her. There was no need for that. This was completely between Andrew and me. For all I knew, the girl probably didn't even know I existed. It's okay to fight for love; however, you should never fight another woman over a man. Andrew clearly chose to create a life with another woman, and he was now her problem, not mine. I look at him and say, "Don't you have an explanation for all this?" He angrily replies, "I owe you nothing! We've been over. Now get out of my house before I call the police!" As I rush down the stairs, I look up and tell him he had better reimburse me for all the wedding expenses or I will see him in court. He chuckles and says, "Ha, good luck with that." He then tells me to wait a second, before tossing me my spare keys and telling me to stay away from his house.

He tells me to call Verizon and said he will be disconnecting my cell phone immediately. Then he calls me a psycho stalker. I had never seen such evil in someone's eyes. At that moment it felt like I was looking at someone else. This person was not the person with whom I had fallen in love with. He was a complete stranger in the blink of an eye. As he displayed his true colors, I realized I did not know this person at all.

I couldn't believe this had just happened. I wanted to scream. I felt like I couldn't breathe. I felt like I had just gotten my heart ripped out of my chest. All my friends thought he might be cheating, but I trusted him and didn't think it could be possible especially not after he spent money towards our wedding. I felt like such a fool for begging him when he clearly lied about his family being racist as an excuse not to get married. What kind of human being does that? I rush out of his house and get into my car. As I drive home with my heart racing like crazy, I call my mother. I yell and curse so loud she had trouble understanding me. I can barely speak. I felt like I had the wind knocked out of me. I'm having a difficult time breathing. My mother tells me to go straight home and that she is on her way to see me.

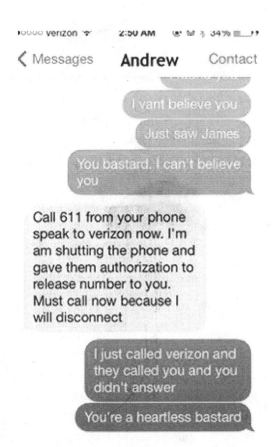

By the time I arrive at my place, my cell phone gets disconnected. Luckily, I had a house phone. As I sit there crying on my mother's shoulder like a baby, I realize a lot of things never added up, and there were a lot of unanswered questions. My mother tells me that she and my father both had their doubts about Andrew being who he said he was. He said he was also a law enforcement officer, yet there was no proof. (In fact, my father went as far as calling him a "Wannabe Zimmerman.")

Andrew always had an excuse for everything. An excuse for why and how he was able to work two full-time jobs; why he didn't keep all his money in his bank accounts; why his last name wasn't Italian, why he "retired" from the police force early at the tender age of 24, etc. The list goes on. I email Andrew telling him that the customer representative was not able to authorize a phone number transfer. He replies back telling me he will call to make the authorization. Finally, after several minutes of registering a new account, I scroll down my phone and block Andrew's phone numbers. I later realized that the whole "funeral" might have been a cover-up and that it had to do with his own racism, bigotry, prejudices, etc. He was looking for an excuse to get out of marrying me and rather than just being upfront, he chose to be cowardly and disgusting.

To top it off, Andrew left it upon me to make all the necessary contacts to cancel the wedding services—catering company, DJ, photographer, wedding coordinator, etc. Can you imagine? After being the one who ended the engagement and betraying me in the way that he did, the coward didn't even have the decency to make a few phone calls. If I didn't have to worry about being financially liable for the expenses, I would have let it all go. Unfortunately, that wasn't the case, so I had no choice but to telephone everyone. I will never forget the evening I received a phone call from the catering manager at the Marina del Rey. He had heard that the contract was terminated and wanted to reach out to me. Apparently, both checks that he had received from Andrew bounced, and the only money he had received was from my father. There were plenty of excuses; however, the catering manager trusted he would eventually get his money, so he was not too concerned.

20

EMPOWERMENT BREAK

Don't ever try to force your happily ever after. Look for signs and pay attention to your gut feeling. If it walks like a duck and quacks like a duck, then it's a duck. Sometimes the one you want to be with is the one you're better off without. Not everyone is meant for everyone - and thank God for that. Stop trying to convince yourself there is hope when you know deep down inside it's over. Often times the answers are right in front of us. We simply seek to ignore them in the hope that things will turn around. Remember, it is your responsibility to define your own worth. Behave as any self-respecting woman would and free yourself from the pain and suffering. You deserve undying loyalty and devotion. If someone ever makes you doubt what you mean to them, then it's time to walk away. A man who truly cares for you will make it clear in his actions and inactions. There will be no 'ifs,' 'buts,' 'ands,' or 'maybe's. If someone walks out of your life, let them. You don't need anyone that doesn't need you. Let go of the need to get an explanation. Their reasons belong to them. Let them keep their opinions. You will more than likely not gain any closure. And that's okay. When someone leaves, that just makes more room for better people. As long as you know the quality of your heart and what kind of person you are, you'll be just fine. Don't shield yourself from the truth no matter how painful it might be. Acceptance can be difficult; however, the truth will always hurt less than a lie in the long run. Learn to accept reality. Denial will prevent you from dealing with your issues and living in peace. Embrace the truth and set yourself free. Real love is not pain. Real love does not lie or cheat.

While it's good that you may not want to give up on people or relationships easily, you should never stay when you know deep in your heart that you deserve more. At the end of the day, it's better to be alone and single than to be unhappy and stuck in the wrong relationship. Once you let go of the wrong people in your life, the right things will start happening.

SECTION 2
The Story of Recovery

Chapter 3

The Pain Is Real

"I don't know why they call it heartbreak. It feels like every other part of my body is broken too." – Terri Guillemets

And the grieving began. My emotions were all over the place. One minute I was angry for having been lied to for so long, the next I felt like my insides were being ripped out. I didn't think it was physically possible to feel so much pain. If I wasn't dying, I almost wanted to. I couldn't understand what I ever did to deserve this kind of betrayal. I was in complete shock. What the hell had just happened? How could this be? How did this happen to me? It felt like just yesterday I was mailing save the dates out and was five months away from marrying the person who I had considered to be not only my best friend, but the love of my life. The next thing I knew, I was single and unsure if I even knew who I had been in a relationship with. Was everything a lie? Did he ever plan on marrying me? Is the girl I saw actually his new fiancé? I began to question everything—the love

I thought we had, his random romantic gestures, etc. "Was it all part of the plan?" I asked myself. So many unanswered questions that I soon learned I would never receive an answer for. The man I had come to know and love never really existed. I was mourning the loss of what was, in fact, a scam. I felt like I got punk'd.

The next moment I was infuriated. He not only wasted my time, but he put my health at risk for God knows how long. I had battled depression on and off for quite some years, but this was by far the worst pain I had ever felt in my entire life. And trust me when I say I had been through a lot prior to this betrayal.

I cried and cried. And when I thought I couldn't possibly cry anymore, I cried even more. I could barely eat. I ended up losing about 15 lbs in less than two weeks. I was weak and exhausted. I couldn't sleep for weeks. And the nights that I did sleep, I dreamt about Andrew. I've never told anyone this until now, but I actually had dreams that everything I saw that night was a complete misunderstanding and that we worked things out. There were mornings I would wake up to realize it was all just a dream, and my heart would ache even more. I was ashamed to still have so much love and hope for someone who had betrayed me so badly. I later started having nightmares that Andrew would be worried I would rat him out for impersonating a law enforcement officer and break into my apartment and shoot me in my sleep. Some may read this and think I'm a bit nuts; however, this wasn't totally far fetched as he did own several guns and after finding out he had been living a double life all along, anything seemed possible. I had no choice to take a personal leave of absence from work. I emailed Andrew asking for the truth as I certainly deserved that at the very least. I told him if he ever cared about me he would at least tell me the truth so that I could gain closure and move on. Well, silence speaks volumes. And silence cuts deeply. He never even had the decency to reply. I had no choice but to let it go. Unfortunately, some people aren't always who you think they are. And that's okay. Don't allow a few bad apples to spoil the bunch. Real love is not pain. Real love does not lie or cheat. Bottom line: If someone starts off the relationship in a lie, it will end in a lie.

Just the thought of Andrew being intimate with another woman was enough to make me feel sick to my stomach. I felt like a fool for not knowing better and being lied to and manipulated in the way I was. A few months after Andrew and I got engaged, I remembered lying in my bed and thinking, "Thank God, I'm off the market and don't have to date all over again." I reflected back on all that I had put up with in the past, and told myself if we were ever to break up, and I had to start all over again with someone new, I would never deal with the same bullshit ever again. I had been such a fool for him. There were a couple of nights when I waited to hear back from him just to have him stand me up, a night when I had prepared dinner and cleaned my house from top to bottom just to have him cancel on me, and even a time when I had my luggage packed ready to go on our first trip, just to have him lie to me about his uncle being sick in the hospital when really he never had our flight and hotel booked. In fact, there were several funerals he supposedly had to attend. Andrew was so good at lying that he could look at you dead in the face and tell you something outrageous, and you'd believe him. What made me really angry was the fact I was not only single again but in my bed crying every night knowing he wasn't. He had someone to go to bed with every night.

I couldn't face my family. I was worried everyone was talking behind my back. What must they think? I was absolutely humiliated. Being "that" girl who actually trusted her man just to be proved that he was not at all who I thought he was.

Everything took place two weeks before Thanksgiving, and I could not bear the thought of sitting at the dining room table being interrogated about what happened. I did not want to be put in the spotlight at a time when I was so fragile that I could burst out into tears at any possible moment. My parents were upset and could not understand my logic and tried to change my mind; however, I stuck to my decision to not be around the family for the holiday. We are so accustomed to spending time with our loved ones during holidays that just the idea (and the actual experience) of being alone during those days created a lot of mental and emotional distress. For me, I felt so emotionally fragile that it was just impossible for me to spend time with my family because I didn't want to make their holidays a sad experience because of my sufferings. I felt a little stronger on Christmas, so I went home. It was still hard, though. New Years came, then Valentine's Day. Never had I imagined to go through back to back holidays single. It was such a hard thing to wrap my mind around. I had planned out the rest of my life with Andrew, and now I was back to square one. I had no idea that my life would come to this.

Despite having dodged a bullet, I was still very much heartbroken when I called off my wedding. After just a couple months, I had some family and friends try to get me to "shake it off." My mother flat out told me Andrew was a "loser" and to just move on. She told me about bad break-ups in our family. She told me about my great aunt being stood up at the church and other aunt's ex-husband who woke up one day and decided he no longer wanted to be married. There was absolutely nothing anyone could say that could make me feel better. Sometimes just listening and being there is enough. Just acknowledging the pain and allowing me to let it all out.

One close friend called me one day and asked me a simple, yet powerful question which completely caught me off guard:

"How long are you going to give yourself to get over it and move on?"

I was stunned. The insensitivity to my heartbreak was hurtful, to say the least. Getting over a serious relationship is easier said than done. Nothing is worse than having your feelings invalidated. Your pain is valid. It hurts because it was real. Don't let anyone take that away from you. If you're hurting, that's okay. It's okay not to be okay. There is no set mourning period or timeline in which you have to get over someone. Allow yourself to feel that pain. Everyone's healing process is different. Take as much time as you need to experience all your emotions so you can heal and move on. While everyone handles hard circumstances differently, your reaction is your choice. It's time to set emotional boundaries and take ownership of your own thoughts and feelings.

When you thought you were going to spend the rest of your life with someone you truly loved, you are going to feel deeply hurt for a while. You don't just stop loving someone because they hurt you. Love doesn't vanish overnight. If it were that easy, all these heartbreak songs, movies, and self-help books wouldn't exist. What you are feeling has been and will be felt by countless others. While people mean well when they give you advice on what they think you should and should not do, you ultimately have to live with the decisions you make.

There comes a point when you just need to let it all out. Allow yourself to have a good cry to wash away all the pain and heartache. Time heals all wounds. Give yourself all the time and space you need to heal, and realize everything will be okay no matter what circumstance comes your way. There's a blessing in the storm. Everyone's circumstance is different. For me, although I appreciated all the love and support, I also had to tune some voices out and do what I knew was best to heal my broken heart. It was my life, and I ultimately had to live with the consequences of my choices, and I wanted to live them on my own. I searched for different outlets—from chatting with other women on message boards to reading books, trying new recipes, etc. Silence and being alone was, in my mind, the best set up for my much-needed healing process. On the other hand, loneliness brought that dreaded toughness of silence and complete awareness of my pain.

But that was a good thing, a painful thing, but good nonetheless. Why? Because it was awareness that brought me the inner strength to not resist my pain anymore. Even though I cannot lie about the fact that the beginning stages of my break-up with Andrew were incredibly painful, it was time and awareness that brought me the knowledge that as long as I kept resisting that pain, suffering would be the inevitable consequence. On the contrary, if I chose to accept and embrace my pain as a welcomed temporary visitor, things would start to feel much different. Suffering started to slowly subside because my attitude towards pain changed. Sufferings and difficulties are a nasty pleasure. They feel terrible, yet they are the true diamonds of life because, if we live them with the right attitude, they are the soil from which our best human qualities can grow and shine.

Our past is an element of life that cannot be changed. We hold no power over it; however, we do hold power over our present. My own suffering and holiday loneliness brought me the incredible realization that it was ultimately up to me to choose how to act and respond to difficult circumstances that come my way. So, with joy in my heart that came from the acceptance of Andrew's betrayal, I reminded myself, as often as I could, that roadblocks and difficulties, though possibly painful, are blessings in disguise. They gave me key lessons and positive personality traits and exactly what I needed at that moment in order to grow. Therefore, I promised myself that from that moment on, anytime I find myself in pain and suffering, I'll ask myself two powerful questions: "What could I learn from this? What's the best attitude I could adopt right now?"

These two questions really put me into a mindset where I practiced the action of embracing my own pain. They brought me acceptance. And not only that, but also gave me an attitude of wanting to find a deep meaning from my own sufferings so that I am worthy of them instead of being a victim of them.

After my initial stage of suffering (which involved a lot of tears, self-victimization, and binge eating), I had to bring out the brave part of myself and face my pain with a long-term solution, which was to embrace my own emotional discomfort as part of my present moment and to stop engaging in actions that made me feel like crap. I realized that I could not incessantly hide behind the temporary solution of quick emotional cover ups.

The aftermath of my break-up with Andrew turned out to be a very healthy one—which was great actually. I figured that the best revenge I could do was to have a killer body! How is that for using pain for improvement? I really didn't want to cover up my pain with quick temporary solutions that pulled me backwards as a person, so improving my fitness was my main physical effort to push forward through these hard times. It kept me focused, with a goal, motivated, and it provided me growth in one of my main pillars in life: health.

Instead of *reacting* with temporary solutions that weren't based on growth, I started to *respond* with an attitude and actions that actually turned me into a better person than I was when I was with Andrew. Because, at the end of the day, if we wish to connect with ourselves and feel happy with life (even when the circumstances are not the desired ones), we have no choice but to give all of our circumstances the highest meaning of all: they are there to teach us something—an opportunity to grow so that we can become even better people. I had no choice but to get up and live again. On what would have been my wedding weekend I instead went away on a girls trip to Miami to celebrate "dodging a bullet." I'll never forget that very morning as I was tidying up before catching my flight. I came across a stack of extra save the dates that I had tucked away. I burst into tears. But what I did next made me feel so much better. I went outside, put the cards on the charcoal grill, and set the save the dates on fire. It felt absolutely amazing. I was saying goodbye to the false promises, goodbye to what could have been, goodbye to settling for less than I deserve. Goodbye and good riddance!

EMPOWERMENT BREAK

All of us experience pain and tragedy we don't always understand. But that doesn't mean things won't get better. Sometimes you have to take matters into your own hands. Don't allow your hardships dictate your life. We are all equipped to handle whatever life throws our way. Even the strongest break. There isn't such thing as a "quick fix" and you may never feel as if you have "recovered," but it does get better, I promise. No matter how bad your heart is broken, you don't have to be miserable forever. The way you think is a choice. You are accountable for making yourself happy. Choose to be an overcomer and find the beauty in the ugliest days. Whatever the mind expects, it finds.

Someone's betrayal is in no way a reflection of the person you are. Know that there was nothing you could have done differently. A good woman can be hard to find. It won't be long before he regrets the day he lost you. Don't let what happened prevent you from moving forward. Realize he did you a favor and thank him for releasing you from a lifetime of unhappiness. You are more than worthy of true love. Everything happens for

33

a reason, and someone better will come along. One day he will no longer cross your mind. The heartache will vanish. There will be no more mourning and crying. Every trace of him will have been removed from your life. No more reminiscing about the past or trying to put the pieces together. All of the confusion and doubt will go away. And suddenly, you don't feel so alone anymore. You recognize the "loss" is, in fact, a gift, and you begin to live again.

Some people come into our lives just to strengthen us so we can move on without them.

It's okay to grieve. In fact, it's vital for your health and well-being. You don't have to put on a brave smile every day. It's okay to let down the walls and cry tears of sorrow. Do what you have to do to heal and move on. Just make sure you don't stay there and drown in self-pity and misery. Life must go on.

After the sadness and anguish of enduring a broken engagement went away, later came the embarrassment and shame. Despite having been betrayed and being the innocent bystander in the situation, I couldn't help but feel that way. It may not make sense to some; however, I felt like a fool for being "that girl" who truly trusted her man and not thinking he was capable of such betrayal. After a lot of self-exploration, I soon came to realize that although a failed relationship can sometimes be humiliating, I should be proud of myself for not only being strong enough to walk away with dignity and grace, but for using the pain as motivation to improve myself. My heart may have been broken, but I'm far from destroyed.

Chapter 4

Clarity

"Sometimes it takes a good fall to really know where you stand." — **Hayley Williams**

There were times, (honestly, there still are times) when it all feels as if I'm telling someone else's story. It was all just surreal. It's a bit difficult putting this dissociation into words, but it was almost like an "out of body" experience if you will. I was numb and confused. "Did this just really happen?" I thought. "Did I just go from engaged to single?" It was all so much to take in. But eventually, reality sunk in and I was able to see things more clearly. I learned that sometimes loss is the only way to grow. Despite being the innocent bystander in the whole ordeal, I had to come to terms with the fact that I was the common denominator in all my past relationships. I kept allowing men into my life who had no respect for me and always made excuses for their unacceptable behavior. I gave chance after chance in hopes that things would eventually change for the better. I had to take responsibility for the changes that needed to be made in me. Once I accepted this harsh truth, I was able to see things more clearly and make the necessary changes to turn my life around.

People stay too long in relationships they shouldn't in fear of being alone. No matter how much they are hurting, they stay in that unhealthy relationship. Sometimes in life, you have to keep on repeating the same mistakes in order for you to learn and grow into a wiser, more confident person. And that was the case for me. I was so hungry for love that I ignored all the red flags and hoped things would work out in my favor. I was so stuck on having a fabulous wedding and finally getting my fairytale ending that I turned a blind eye to hurt and pain.

Despite the heartbreak, I now know that every person who comes into your life teaches you a lesson. Sometimes we learn more about ourselves from the people who cause us pain. We learn through experience what our insecurities are, the importance of listening to our instincts, and what we value in relationships. I have no regrets. I wouldn't change what happened. It is better to be single and alone than taken for granted. Better to be alone than with someone who makes you feel alone.

After much reflection, I realized I had always put Andrew on such a high pedestal and never truly valued myself. I ignored his shortcomings and convinced myself I wouldn't find anyone better. While there were certain aspects of his personality that had always bothered me, I let it all go and tried to focus on the positive. After all, as I said before, he appeared to be so great "on paper" that I felt like, if anything, I would be able to help him in the areas he lacked. I thought my love for him was strong enough to carry us through anything and everything that came against us. The truth is, no woman can change a man unless he himself wants to change.

Looking back at my history, I realized that in retrospect, I had brought this all upon myself. Growing up, I had always been very shy, and when I say shy, I mean *painfully* shy. I could barely order a meal at a restaurant, let alone speak up for myself and what I believed in. Now here I'm being extremely vocal about my thoughts and opinions and sharing the most intimidate details of my broken engagement to everyone. Time truly turns us into a better person if we choose to learn instead of asking "why me?" I finally found my voice which has improved every aspect of my life. No longer do I take it personally when someone misjudges me, no longer do I rely on anyone to make me happy, no longer do I put my needs and wants on the back burner. And no longer do I allow anyone to make me feel unworthy or insignificant. Now that I know better, I do better.

As I said before, I placed little value on myself and a much higher one on Andrew. I felt so thirsty for love that I wanted to hold on to him because I didn't feel worthy of anything better. How silly, right? Thankfully, now I can see much better now. I can see that it is impossible to have a quality man in my life if I don't consider myself a very high-quality woman. It doesn't matter who you are or what you may or may not have been through. Every woman should always acknowledge her worth and should work on expanding it daily. She knows which are the main areas of her life, her pillars, and makes a conscious and directed effort to recognize where she's at in every one of them and what she can do on an ongoing basis to improve them.

Emotionally independence is a must. A woman should never seek love from others in order to feel fulfilled. She understands that the main source of love is the inner love she nurtures in her own heart every day. She takes care of herself the same way she would take care of her child, not only physically but also spiritually, mentally and emotionally.

Have you noticed how mothers pour their best love into their children? Well, we can pour the same love to ourselves because it comes from our inner-self. In reality, even though we enjoy a great sense of purpose and deep love from a relationship with a wonderful man, we can only enjoy and offer the best in our relationships when our emotional maturity is grounded in deep self-love.

EMPOWERMENT BREAK

Some see relationships as investments and find it difficult to "throw it all away." You have to decide what you truly want. Does being together make you happy? Does he bring out the best in you? Are you emotionally and physically safe at all times? On the surface, you may feel loved and have the companionship you craved, but at what price? Would you rather experience temporary pain or have a lifetime of unhappiness? It's your choice. I'm not going to pretend that it's easy because I know it's not. Leaving a relationship is never easy. The fact of the matter is you have to learn to reframe your thoughts around your circumstance and see the positive side of change. You do not have to live in regret. Maybe you're wondering, "How could I be so foolish?" Or, "I should have known better." Stop that. The truth is: You can't help who you love. It's not your fault you gave all your love to someone who wasn't worthy. It's what you do now that counts. We as women hold incredible power—we have strength and resilience. Honor your gut instinct and do what feels right to you. Everyone goes through trials and tribulations. It's up to you to choose to let them guide you and apply the lessons learned.

Chapter 5

Moving On, Growing Closer To God

"Nothing happens to you, it happens for you."
– Joel Olsteen

There were times when I came very close to losing my faith completely. I had so many nights where I cried out to God and asked, "Why me? Why did this happen to me? I'm a good person. What did I ever do to deserve this kind of pain?" I had been through so much in the past, and honestly, some days it fathoms me how I've even made it this far.

When we were casually dating, I prayed every night that God would make Andrew and me a couple. And when we finally became an item, I thanked Him constantly for blessing me with a great partner in life. And after the betrayal? Well, I prayed even harder that He would help heal my broken heart and help ease the pain. I felt like I was cursed. I'm far from perfect, but my heart is pure and my intentions are good; however, I felt like bad things always happened to me. I could never seem to catch a break.

It took a long time, but I'm so thankful God did not answer some of my prayers as those unanswered prayers have led me to the place I'm meant to be. I'm beyond grateful for the tears, the heartache, and the sleepless nights. If it weren't for my troubles, I would have never found my strength. Although we sometimes feel like some things are so unfair, the reality is that tough times are simply just part of life. Like a rollercoaster, life has its high points and low points, and you have to see a few low points in order to get to the high ones. But during those low points in life, it's hard to ever imagine that things are going to get better. Yet it's during these times you must stay strong and have faith that all things happen for a reason, and you will get through it. Hardships like health scares, financial problems and break-ups fall on everyone. But it's during those hard times that the power of faith can help restore your spirit and help drag yourself out from those low points and see the light at the end of the tunnel. Even though you might feel as if you'll never be happy again, you must keep the faith that things are going to get better or else you'll fall into a downward spiral of depression and lose all hope, especially when you fall out of love with someone you thought was going to be your soul mate. Suffering is unavoidable, so the best thing you can do is learn from it and push through the pain. Know that everything happens for a reason and have faith that one day you'll realize why you had to suffer. Learn and grow from what you've learned and believe that something better is going to come out of it. Believe that this hardship will shed light on what life's purpose is for you. Although it may be hard to follow your faith, remember that it's the hope that will get your out of this hardship. Without it, you might never heal, so be positive and try not to follow your feelings so much, despite how hard that may be. Base your decisions during hard times on your faith—whether that's God, the universe or some other higher power—because that's what will help you grow and reach those high points in life. When you have faith, you believe in a higher power, and that's what will help you find strength during tough times. Believing that things will get better and staying positive will help you realize that it's for the better, and something good will later come from this. You just have to be patient to realize what that good is.

After my engagement came to an end, I really learned that faith and spirituality are truly important and should be the foundation for all things in your life. People will come in and out of your life. If you are hurting now, know that it will eventually pass. Everything's coming together—even though it doesn't seem that way. There are no coincidences in life. Every chapter of your life has already been written. Whether times are good or bad, it's important to realize that nothing happens to you, it happens for you. Every disappointment and every struggle is a blessing in disguise.

When put in perspective, breaking up with someone is probably not the worst thing that could happen to you. But while you're in the situation and experiencing all this pain, it often feels like you'll never be able to move on. I know how much it hurts. Life is meant to be shared, and when you've been ready to share yours with someone and they choose to let you go, it's the ultimate rejection. You start thinking you're not worthy of love; you're not worthy of anything. You spend your nights alone, crying, and the worst part is that you prefer it that way. Why go out?

Why face the world? What's the point?

If this is how you're feeling right now, or even if you've overcome it partly but still hold grudges, it's time to heal. I know it's a cliché, but life is indeed too short and too beautiful to miss out. "But how?" you're probably thinking to yourself. Simple— through daily spirituality and gratitude practice. Unfortunately, spirituality and all practices related to it are still overlooked by many, but if you sit down and really talk with people, you'll realize most non-believers have never tried it or have tried it once. For spirituality to get to you, especially if you haven't been connected to yourself in that way before, it takes time *and* work. Just as with anything else, practice makes perfect.

EMPOWERMENT BREAK

You can start small—just take a few minutes of your day to focus on all the great things in your life. And there are great things in your life for sure! Maybe it's your family and friends. Maybe it's the fact that you're blessed to live in an amazing country, city or neighborhood. Or maybe it's your job that gives you joy. There's always something. Focusing on all the amazing things you do have in your life instead of not having that one person (seriously, it's just one person, and it's not like there's a shortage of humans on Earth) will completely change your state.

And changing your state will change the decisions you take, which will change everything else.

The next step would be spending some time meditating. Meditation is different than visualizations and gratitude practices. While during visualization and gratitude practices you focus, respectively, on what you want and on what you have, meditation lets you focus on yourself. Meditation is not difficult, not at all, but it does require some patience and inner peace. Just sitting comfortably, focused on your breath, letting your mind wander while gently letting go of recurring thoughts will give you a deep awareness and understanding of who you are, what truly bothers you, and how to overcome it.

Because let me tell you right now—your subconscious mind is a genius and all you need to do to handle any challenging situation is let it lead you. That's precisely what spirituality practices are about—they bring out the genius, the God inside of you and let him or her take the decisions for a change.

And really, who would prefer to think about the person that rejected them when you can find your inner God instead?

Chapter 6

Letting Go Of Toxic Relationships

"Letting go means to come to the realization that some people are a part of your history, but not a part of your destiny."
—Steve Maraboli

Some people are simply meant to be in your life for a season. I personally did a major purge of friends in the past few years because they were unhealthy for me (whether their habits, outlooks, dependency, or something else), and it was difficult when they contacted me to see how I was doing. I sometimes hesitated and debated whether or not I should respond to calls or text messages, but then I reminded myself that I had to remain conscious of the initial reasons we "split." I have recognized that when I become the only one reaching out to help them (and they expect that), or that how they reach out to me is not conducive to my own life, then something needs to change.

It is essential that you learn to accept the fact that everyone may not have the same compassion in their hearts as you. Once you realize this, you can start changing the way in which you respond to people. A true friend or partner will not take advantage of you and treat you like a doormat. You don't need to change to be accepted. You need to change what you're willing to accept from other people. Never compromise yourself, what you believe in, what you stand for, etc. Set boundaries so that people understand what line not to cross. Have standards so that you know exactly what you will and will not tolerate. Value yourself and know when to pull the plug. Not everyone deserves to have you in their life, and not everyone needs to be friends.

Change is an inevitable part of life, and the truth of the matter is throughout your journey in life, you will lose and gain many people. The good news is the people who are meant to be in your circle will always be there. Even if they may disappear for a bit, they will gravitate back to you at the most unexpected time. Timing is truly everything.

I have some friends who I can go months, maybe even a year without talking to them; however, when we do reconnect, it's as though we literally just picked up where we left off. I consider these people my true friends. Then there are those that choose to communicate with me when it is convenient for them. Friends who will disappear and reappear at any given notice. Absolutely no contact no matter how hard I reach out, but then suddenly, they will come back into my life as though nothing had happened. This has always boggled my mind. Am I supposed to welcome these type of "friends" with open arms? Unfortunately, the reality of the matter is people have different expectations of what true friendship is all about and often do no reciprocate the same kindness and respect you show them. Their behavior is disrespectful and needs to be recognized as such.

With some old friends, I was flat out honest and made a clean break. I recall letting one particular friend know about my feelings about our friendship. As you can imagine, it did not go that well. People tend to take things quite personally when you call them out on ummm...bullshit? It is what it is. I had never felt so empowered speaking my truth and telling it how it is. It's not always easy when you genuinely care about the person; however, it is absolutely liberating.

Other friendships just "fizzled out" over time and we've become acquaintances. Life happens and friendships change over the years. People get busy with their careers, get married, have children, move across the country, etc. It's not always easy to keep in touch with everyone. And that's okay.

And other friendships simply ended without even explanations. That's right. I had about two "good" friends go cold turkey and end contact with me without evening having the courtesy to have a conversation with me about whatever made them come to their decisions. Honestly, as much as it bothered me that they both didn't even feel the need to hash things out, I knew deep down that if they were able to dismiss me in such a way, that they did not even deserve a word from me. Why chase after anyone who voluntarily decides to walk out of your life? I've always had enough pride in myself to know that "rejection" is not always a bad thing. Why chase after anyone who voluntarily decides to walk out of your life?

Then there are those people who only spend time and communicate with you when it is convenient for them. They pick and choose when they want to contact you, when they want to respond to you, etc. I don't know about you, but I personally don't have time for any of that nonsense. Not everyone deserves to be in your life. When you go through tough moments in life, that's when you know who your true friends are. After calling off my wedding I learned who my true friends were by looking around at who was there for me and who wasn't.

At the end of the day, there is not a single friendship from the past that I would take back. I'm content with those who are in my life and know they are aligned with my values and beliefs. Are there sometimes some people I'm unsure of? Absolutely. I would be lying if I said there weren't a few people I'm somewhat unsure of. I try to give people the benefit of the doubt. However, I assure you, the moment I feel disrespected and taken for granted, I will cut all ties without warning.

Sometimes we have a tendency to explain and reaffirm ourselves to others, but why? Do we really need to do this? What is our true motive behind our search of reassurance from others? Living in a society where we are in constant interaction with others, having other people not understand us can make us feel a disconnect that can be difficult to bear, and hence our need to "help others understand us." Although this may be helpful sometimes, at the end of the day, everything that we do in our lives has to come from a deep inner feeling of self-love. This disconnect I mentioned before is, in a way, a lack of love. We all want to feel loved and accepted. The truth is no external love will ever be enough, no matter how often we receive it, if our own inner love is not well established. Our need of being accepted, of feeling loved, cannot be based on other people's opinions about ourselves. The healthiest belief a human being can have in order to not fall into this trap is:

"Other people's opinions can be helpful and important, but they are never more important than the most important opinion of the world: my opinion."

Setting healthy boundaries and saying 'no' when 'no' is the most loving answer one can give comes as a natural step from the above belief. We value our self-love as one of our most precious treasures, which automatically translates into giving that love back to others.

Having a personal set of relationship deal-breakers is crucial as you want to always make sure your core values and beliefs align with those of the person you are in a relationship with. Everyone has their own personal deal-breaker when it comes to what they absolutely won't tolerate in a relationship. There are just some things that will set a person over the edge and declare a relationship over.

Over time, they can and will change. You may come to realize that what you once perceived to be a deal-breaker was actually something you could learn to live with, and you could simply agree to disagree. On the other hand, your last relationship may have been that "wake up call" you needed for you to come to realize that you didn't value yourself or know your standards. This is also known as having "non-negotiables." These are traits and characteristics that disqualify a potential dating prospect, regardless of many great traits they may have. Although everyone has different deal-breakers, there are some major ones every woman should have. For instance, no form of abuse should ever be tolerated. There is only so much a person can forgive, but when it comes to abuse, that is completely unacceptable. Whether it's physical or emotional abuse, no woman should ever, under any circumstances, date an abusive person. Being in an abusive relationship is never good, so if there are any signs of abuse at the beginning of a relationship, then it's time to axe that person from your life or else you're in for a rocky and sad relationship.

You'd think that no woman ever would choose to spend even a minute of her valuable time with a man that can't take care of his health, but nuh-uh! Almost every day I notice beautiful ladies with poorly groomed men with bad breath and dirt beneath their nails. Girls! Wake up! You deserve so much more than that. If he can't even take care about his look and his health, how will he ever be able to take care of you and your future family?

Another no-brainer is cheating. No self-respecting woman would want to date a cheater and here's news for you—if a guy is known to be a cheater, you can't change him! I repeat, you can't change him! So don't waste your time.

And what about a guy who can't take responsibility? It's weird how some women don't notice that until it's too late. They fall for a man with a charming smile and miss the fact that he has no job, no car and still lives with his parents. If you want to be a babysitter, that's fine, but don't be one in your relationship.

Last but not least, you should never be with a man who would rather spend a night out with the boys than a night at home with you. I don't mean keeping your man locked up at home, but there are some fellas out there who'd choose their freedom over a healthy relationship any day. Stay away from them, they don't deserve you.

Andrew always made me believe it was my problem when he was the entire problem. It is the way he emotionally manipulated me to get his way and to be able to continue to lie, and cheat. By deflecting blame onto me, he kept the power. He had the ability to have the upper hand and continued to do all the negative and abusive actions he chose to do.

EMPOWERMENT BREAK

You gotta know when to hold 'em and when to fold 'em.

It's normal to miss people. However, just because you may miss someone, doesn't mean they belong in your life. Not all relationships are meant to last forever. Not everyone you lose is a loss. Sometimes, some people just aren't meant to be in your life. This goes for both friendships and romantic relationships. So, ladies, it's important to set boundaries as to what you will and won't tolerate so that you don't end up being stuck in a relationship or friendship you're going to hate later on!

SECTION 3

Love in Romance & with You

Chapter 7

Co-Dependency

"We are Lovable. Even if the most important person in your world rejects you, you are still real, and you are still okay."
— Melody Bettie

*B*eing in a relationship can be a wonderful thing. Having someone to love, do things with, share yourself with and do things for can be quite fulfilling for many women. But when does it cross the line of being too much? Some women lose themselves in relationships and forget about putting their own needs first because they're too wrapped up in being everything for their partner. They lose sight of who they are because they're giving their all to make their partner happy, often losing friendships, sleep and more over trying to make their partner happy 24/7. This is unhealthy, as it may cause us pain down the road if the relationship doesn't work out. If you never learn to love yourself before the other person, it may be hard to accept the loss and move on from them. When a woman is too caught up in her romantic relationships, this can be a form of co-dependency.

As a behavioral and emotional condition, co-dependency can affect a woman's ability to have a healthy and mutually satisfying relationship. Many define it as having a "relationship addiction" because people who have co-dependency issues often have relationships that are one-sided, destructive and even abusive. They love being in a relationship, even though it might be unhealthy for them, and fail to break it off no matter how destructive it may be. Co-dependency is thought to be a learned behavior, and it can be passed down from generations. Women can learn to be co-dependent by watching their mothers, aunts or other important female figures in their lives who display this type of behavior.

To put it in simple terms, co-dependency is when you are so invested in any relationship that you can't function as an independent person anymore. Everything you do and feel is defined by that other person with whom you are so involved that you lose your own identity. In this type of relationship, there is a passive participant who looks to the dominant person for decisions. And it's the stronger personality that gets some kind of satisfaction from the fact that they can control the other person knowing that they are the center of their world.

When I was with Andrew, I was on such a mission to "earn" my ring that I was willing to compromise anything and everything to ensure that it came to fruition. I was always willing to drop anything and everything to spend time with him. I cancelled plans with friends so that I could see him instead, made excuses for not being able to go out—heck I'm sure I even didn't make any plans a few times in hopes that he would want to see me. I made him my world and told myself that as long as I had him in my life, I was good.

Ladies, you cannot, and should not put your life on hold for anyone. It's okay to spend time with yourself or your friends, instead of your partner. Not only will this help you separate yourself from your "other half," but your friends will appreciate seeing you sometimes without your boyfriend tagging along. People act differently when they are alone with friends than when they have their significant other with them. Someone should be *part* of your world, not your *entire* world. If you do that, and that person is no longer in your life, what are you left with?

Nothing.

Wondering if you are, in fact, in a co-dependent relationship? There are some major signs that you should be aware of if you are wondering if you might have co-dependency issues.

The first one is fear of abandonment. Are you so afraid that your loved one will leave you that you try to do everything for them so that stay? Co-dependency is when you fear being alone and do anything you can to make your loved one stay. Next is a need for approval. Everything you do needs to be validated by your significant other. Your worth is not tied to any person. Don't attach your value to what someone may or may not think.

Low self-esteem is another factor. Do you suffer from low self-esteem and lack trust in yourself? Not seeing your worth can be a sign of co-dependency. You are the only one who can control how you feel. Don't depend on anyone for your happiness. Low self-confidence can and does kill relationships and limit your ability to meet anyone new.

Do you ever have difficulty making decisions and identifying your feelings? Realize that, over time, if you let your partner make all the decisions and don't like to speak up about how you feel about things, you're being too dependent on your partner. Communication is key to a healthy relationship and when you don't have that, things can start to go south; especially when you don't want to speak up, fearing that your partner might get angry and upset with you.

It can often be hard sometimes for people to learn to love themselves despite what is going on in their social lives, and sometimes this can be even more of a problem when it comes to being in a relationship. It is time to take responsibility for yourself. Don't blame yourself for someone else's troubles or wrongdoings. Instead, you need to start putting yourself first and not your partner. As a co-dependent woman, you need to learn how to break off from the destructive relationship and find yourself once and for all. You are not defined by anyone but yourself, and that responsibility starts with you and you only. Loving yourself first improves your self-esteem which can and does affect the way others connect with you. Being more negative, if you have low self-esteem, could actually damage your relationship.

To break co-dependency, you have to realize that you are your own person, and your entire being isn't about making everyone else happy, but making yourself happy. You need to start taking responsibility for yourself and that entails making your own choices and doing things that make you happy, regardless of how your partner feels. It is so important that you work to end the recurring self-destructive patterns that lead you there in the first place. You need to take steps to avoid these self-sabotaging habits, and although it won't happen overnight, it can be done with patience and determination.

First and foremost, you have to realize that there's a problem in your relationship. When you avoid the fact that there's a problem, you're in denial and will continue on the path to self-destruction and your co-dependency issues. Look at the problem and acknowledge it in your current relationship and those from the past. Understand that it can change and make a conscious effort to want to change.

The second step is to change one step at a time. You're not going to go from co-dependency to an independent woman overnight, so when you're ready to change, pick one thing at a time. Start with investing time in yourself and doing things that make you happy. Then work on accepting being alone and gradually work your way up to living an independent life—whether it's in a relationship or on your own.

Be committed. The change will happen over time as long as you are committed. Don't give up when things get hard. And if your partner isn't supporting your change and continue to try to have you being dependent on them, it's time to rethink the relationship. Remember, it's about being a happy and independent woman who doesn't need a man in her life to define who she is. It may be hard to do, but you have to stay committed to wanting to change, even if it means leaving the relationship.

To help with your co-dependency issues when you go into new relationships, you'll need to establish boundaries for yourself and your partner. This means recognizing when you're giving your all into a one-sided relationship. It also means establishing things you will and won't do in a relationship, including not allowing yourself to think that your partner is your world and losing your identity.

Don't seek affirmation or comforting words from others, but rather learn to tell yourself those things that you like about yourself. Not only will this teach you to appreciate yourself, but it will also prevent annoying others by constantly seeking compliments.

EMPOWERMENT BREAK

The fact of the matter is someone else loving you doesn't equal loving yourself. It is important to work on loving yourself, or working on making yourself someone that you do love, whether or not someone else already loves you. We often let our significant other "complete" us, and if they are happy with us, nothing else matters. However, it is important to remind yourself that someone else's love is not a reason to stop seeking out your own happiness with yourself. Don't let your partner shape the future you have in mind for yourself. Although a little com-

promise is important in a relationship, don't change yourself or ignore your feelings because it's what the other person wants and you are afraid of losing them. This will help you set goals for yourself without the help of your partner so that you know what you want out of life to be fulfilled.

Co-dependency can ruin your relationships and cause you to be a person you never wanted to be. Finding hobbies or interests that you don't have in common with your partner is also very important. You have to be your own person and have your own identity separate from your partner. Don't try to convince someone to become interested in your hobbies, and don't force yourself to become interested in theirs. Embrace that there are things that you do without each other, and keep doing them. This will provide an easy opportunity to detach yourself from your partner, which will allow you to remain your own independent person.

The good news in all of this is that you can break away from these unhealthy habits and become an independent woman. Co-dependency is not a death sentence. If you apply the skills *you learn from this chapter, you can and will emerge from it all and create a new, healthy mindset that is congruent with your values and intent.*

Chapter 8

Forgiveness

"True forgiveness is when you can say, 'Thank you for that experience.'" —Mahatma Gandhi

*S*ometimes it may be difficult to move on and not feel the need to seek revenge because we are deeply hurt by the ones that are closest to us. It is difficult to understand why people do the things they do.

Don't worry. I'm not going to lie to you and say I wanted him to find what or who makes him happy. In fact, I wanted revenge. I wanted sweet, sweet revenge. I wanted to pull a Carrie Underwood and slash his tires. I even had friends offer to help me vandalize his car. I thought of every legal way that I could possibly bring great pain and humiliation to him. But in the end, I didn't act on any of those thoughts. As much as I wanted to "get even" for all of the pain and anguish he had caused me, I decided it just wasn't worth it. Even though all of the wedding expenses had gone straight down the drain and I was not the least bit financially stable on my own, I quickly realized that you can't put a price on inner peace. Life is about so much more than money. And if I was only out a few thousand dollars (and some tears), I considered myself lucky to have my health and be in control of my happiness. Five thousand dollars to dodge a bullet and prevent myself from having a lifetime of unhappiness is priceless if you ask me.

Why be bitter when you can do better? Give yourself another chance to find love and happiness. The only thing you can do is set yourself free of the burden. Life is way too short to waste holding onto hate and anger. Don't you agree? No matter how deeply someone may have hurt you, it is important to let go of that desire to get revenge. Trust me; I know that it isn't always easy. However, when you let go and redirect your energy to the things and people that you love the most, you will gain a serene inner peace that will be far more satisfying. After all, happiness really is the best revenge. I'm so very thankful to have not had kids with someone so hateful and that I finally found out who he truly was before our lives became even more entangled.

Now I would like to present you with a piece of advice based on my own personal experiences in both life and love. Whatever you do, never allow your wounds to turn you into someone you're not. Instead, choose to take the high road and move on with dignity and grace. As I previously mentioned, this may not always be easy, but nothing worthwhile is easy, and it's the only way to find inner peace and happiness again. If you find yourself beginning to feel down or start blaming your own actions, reactions and words for the falling out or break_up, you need to break out of the victim mentality and choose another path. You know very well what you need to do. Simply let karma take care of the revenge. You can hold your head up high knowing that those who hurt you will eventually face their own karma.

You also need to find it within yourself to forgive the people who have wronged you. Just because you forgive someone for mistreating you, doesn't mean you condone the hurt they may have caused you. Forgiveness can and will lead to healing and the releasing of emotional baggage, but it may take a little time. Eventually, the practice of forgiveness will allow you to gain peace in order to move forward in your life. Also, you need to learn to forgive yourself and keep in mind that wisdom comes from failure. Our biggest failures build character, confidence, and strength. So, stay focused, consistent, and diligent if you want to get your life back. Remember that patience is a virtue and just because it's not happening now, doesn't mean it never will.

In order to forgive and move on, you will want to make it a point to not let any old feelings linger around. I know it seems hard at times to lay everything on the table, leave it there and walk away; however, you can't move forward in life if you're holding onto old baggage. Go ahead. Give yourself permission to let go of the past. Letting go of grudges and bitterness is the only way you will be able to bring peace and contentment back into your life.

Reframing your thoughts around your circumstances truly does wonders. Your words are more powerful than you think, so it is so very important that you learn to speak words of kindness to yourself. Bitterness can and will imprison you. Rephrase negative thoughts and statements with positive ones and try your best to see both sides of the situation.

It took me some time for me to get to a place where I was genuinely able to forgive Andrew. After a long period of anguish, I was able to accept the fact that what happened, happened and I just had to move on. Today, I can honestly say I would like to thank him.

Andrew, thank you for breaking my heart. Thank you for waking me up to what I had foolishly turned a blind eye to for so long. Thank you for letting me go and giving me the opportunity to find someone else. Thank you for teaching me the importance of loving myself first. There really is always a good in goodbye. Who knew heartbreak would be the most precious gift? I'm no longer consumed by the pain. The heartache is over, and the tears are long gone. The thought of you, and what could have been no longer brings a lump to my throat. Thank you for showing me that life can and does go on without you. And that it is much, much sweeter. Thank you, thank you, thank you.

EMPOWERMENT BREAK

I also strongly believe that you must learn to forgive yourself. After all, you are your longest commitment. Stop beating yourself up for past mistakes and failures. Concentrate on the good things. There's a lesson in everything. One day you will thank God for those who walked out of your life. Give yourself permission to learn and grow. Take a deep breath and savor this moment.

Congratulations. You are one step closer to discovering your purpose and becoming your happiest self. Now that you know what you need to do to forgive and get on with your life, put a smile on your face and do it! Don't look back. Once you get over the hurdle of forgiveness, everything else will come easier. Just remember to surround yourself with those who have only the best intentions for you and your future. Sometimes all you need is a good support system to help you out.

Chapter 9

Taming Your Fear

"Thinking will not overcome fear but action will."
—W. Clement Stone

*D*espite what some people may tell you, breaking up is never an easy thing to do. This is mainly because you have to sort through all of the guilt, the doubt and the fear you are left with after a bad break-up before you move on to find someone else you want to share your life with. Well, if you are ever going to love again, you are going to need to learn how to tame your relationship fears. There are some things you need to do in order to regain your independence, let go of the past and put your best foot forward into the future of life, love, and happiness.

Trust is vital in any relationship, whether it be friendship or a romantic relationship. If you have been cheated on, trust can be a fragile thing. Once trust is broken, it almost can never be repaired.

You will always second guess something, over analyze, and stress yourself out. Whatever you do, try not to let past mistrust destroy a new relationship. Tackling any trust issues that you might have developed or increased after the break-up should be one of the first matters you address. It's easy to assume that everyone is out to hurt you or play with your feelings once you have gone through a terrible break-up, but this mistrust is of course misplaced. This is why it is important to remember that you were hurt by just one person, and there are still many trustworthy people in the world. If you feel you can trust him, you shouldn't overthink it or become obsessed with the idea of him possibly betraying you. Once you learn to divert your mistrust to only one person, you can open your heart and mind to the idea of letting in someone new.

The next step of the healing process is to overcome any fear or self-doubt that you may have. If you fear the idea of getting into a new relationship because of the hurt you experienced when your last one ended, you're going to need to get over this. Instead of doubting yourself when it comes to love and relationships, work on building your confidence by discovering the things that make you unlike anyone else. This will help build your confidence and banish any self-doubt that may be lingering around.

When you're in a lengthy relationship and then it suddenly ends, it's easy to get stuck in an emotional box. If you want to finally move on with your life, you're going to have to step outside of that box and get way out of your comfort zone. You can start by doing something you have never done before, going somewhere you have never gone before or accepting a date proposition from someone you probably never would have considered a few years ago. You never know what you will find when you open yourself up to new experiences, new scenery or new feelings.

It is in our nature as human beings to want things to go perfectly when it comes to our relationships, but perfection does not exist in reality. Failure is a natural part of life and you should begin accepting it. For this reason alone, you are going to need to learn how to let go of perfectionism in order to prevent severe disappointment when things don't go your way. A few ways you can teach yourself how to let go of perfectionism is by setting realistic expectations, compartmentalizing and practicing self compassion. Let yourself fail, accept it, and learn from the experience.

Change is inevitable in our personal lives, our career lives and our love lives, which is why you are just going to have to embrace it. Instead of freaking out and freezing when change occurs, simply pull yourself up and roll with the punches. We are not always going to live up to our own expectations. That's just the reality.

EMPOWERMENT BREAK

One way to embrace change is to make the change. For example, you could look at moving to a new place, updating your hairstyle, losing weight or making new friends. Regularly making these small changes in your life will prepare you to better handle the big changes in life that are less frequent, but often times more devastating on your daily comforts.

If you have ever doubted yourself or feared getting back into the dating world, you should keep in mind that you are definitely not alone. In fact, fear is quite a common emotion among both men and women who have just gone through a difficult breakup or divorce. Your ability to bounce back after a break-up can play a crucial role in your overall quality of life, so you shouldn't ever ignore your feelings. Face them head on, get over it and get on with your life.

Chapter 10

Self-Love In Romantic Relationships

"Don't wander away from yourself to get close to someone else." —Unknown

*L*ove. We want it; we need it. We so desperately want to be loved by others that we go to the ends of the Earth to find it. Unfortunately, so many women fail to understand that you must be your own first love. The moment you truly realize the magnificent being you are, you won't accept anything less than the absolute best from another person. As women, we need to learn to commit to loving and respecting ourselves before we're able to accept love from others. A man learns how to treat a woman based on how she treats herself. This is why it's of utmost importance that you always carry yourself in a manner worthy of dignity and respect. Others will pick up on this self-confidence and in turn, respect who you are as a person, loving you the same way you love yourself.

People make time for what they value. We often make excuses for others and hope they will change. The truth is if they do not see your value, then they simply aren't deserving of your time. Stop looking outside of yourself for your value. Respect yourself and value your worth. You don't need other people to validate you. You are already valuable! Once you realize this, you'll automatically see a difference in how people will see and react to you. It all starts with you and knowing your value.

Learning to stand on your own two feet and taking responsibility for yourself is how to gain self-love. Putting yourself first and realizing what you want from your life and your relationships allows you to strengthen your self-love so that you can radiate it out to the world. Never put your wants and needs on the back burner. Don't ever compromise your standards. You can't control someone else's behavior; however, you can control what you condone.

One of the most important relationships you will have throughout your life is the one with yourself. While all others will come and go, the relationship that you have with yourself will never fail. Learn to celebrate yourself. Believe that you are good. Be proud of your gifts and talents and what you have achieved.

Love yourself unconditionally and love will naturally find you. You will exude an energy that is not only contagious, but also completely irresistible. Others will see a difference in how you carry yourself and will instantly be attracted to you since they can feel how comfortable you are in your own skin. You're not trying to hide anything or be something you're not. Confidence is attractive and others will gravitate to you once you finally realize your self-love.

Ladies, always know your worth. Don't ignore those red flags. If it's meant to be, it will be. Don't try to push something to work or else you'll just make the problem worse. Love shouldn't be hard and should flow naturally. Anything else isn't meant to be. But in order to realize this, you have to first realize the love you have for yourself. You have to know that you are truly worth more and should be given more from your partners. Settling for anything less than that will compromise your relationship with yourself. And the more the relationship with yourself is wrecked, the harder it is to find your way back to yourself. Don't let it get to that point. Continue loving yourself through the hard times and the good, and don't ever let anyone take that self-love away from you.

Follow your heart, but take your brain with you. Don't let your heart rule you. At the end of the day, it's better to be alone and single than to be unhappy and stuck in the wrong relationship. You'll not only be happier in the long run, but you'll come to realize how much you better off you are without them—despite the hurt in the beginning. And once you finally relieve yourself of them, you're allowing new love to enter your life. Once you let go of the wrong people in your life, the right things will start happening.

Know what you stand for and what you won't stand for. Dig deep and really know yourself. If someone is mistreating you on an ongoing basis, it's time to take that power away from them. Simmering in silence is not going to change anything. You condone what you allow. Speak up for yourself when you're being stepped on. People can't walk all over you if you are standing up for yourself.

When you have experienced great pain, it can be difficult to remain positive; however, know that you control your attitude and outlook on life situations. Find the strength and willpower to move forward and understand that it takes time. Go ahead and grieve, feel sad and be mad. After all, it's important to realize your emotions. But give yourself a set time to mourn the relationship or what you've lost and then promise yourself that you'll move on and put it behind you. Realize that right now is a new beginning. You can still put the pieces back together. Everything you go through grows you. To help get your mind off things and put you in a positive mindset, get involved with things that inspire you or that you're passionate about. And if you don't know what they are, go out and find them! Many turn to exercise to help them feel better, while others might like to bike, run, read, cook or do whatever pleases them. Not only are you allowing yourself positive distractions, but you're also doing something for yourself. You're putting yourself first and are actively seeking to better yourself.

A healthy relationship starts off with the one you have with yourself. Once you have self-love, you'll be able to have the right romantic love. One that doesn't hurt and only brings joy. You'll be able to have a healthy relationship, which is based on reciprocity, mutual respect, and fairness. Don't allow yourself to be a doormat in any relationship, including the one with yourself. Always keep your standards high and never forget that the relationship you have with yourself is the most important one of all.

Chapter 11

Self-Love With You Alone

"To love oneself is the beginning of a life-long romance."
—Oscar Wilde

*I*t's often easier to love someone else than it is to love your-self. For some reason or another, we can freely love others, but when it comes to ourselves, we don't do the same. We put ourselves down and pinpoint all of our flaws, allowing ourselves to self-loathe. We rarely give ourselves the credit we deserve despite the fact that dozens of studies and research show that if we treat ourselves with the same kindness we provide to others, we'd actually live happier and healthier lives.

Self-love is all about giving attention, care, and love to your-self, and in order to have successful relationships with others. It all starts with self-love. We are the only ones responsible for our choices, actions and the outcomes from those choices and actions.

We can't give someone else what we don't have. How are you supposed to really love someone else when you don't have that same love for yourself? Whatever love you say you have for others is nothing but a lie when you don't have it yourself.

Having self-love is vital because it's matched to our power. Self-love puts the power in your hands and is the only way to have boundaries. It's how we learn to say no to things that conflict with our own self-love.

It starts with "me" and allows you to gauge the world around it. It allows you to ask questions if others are truly right for you. When you're confused or in a situation that questions your self-love, you have to stop and ask yourself, "If I truly loved myself, what would I do?"

It's great to think of self-love as the foundation to a full and happy life. It's the single and most important relationship that you'll ever have. To love yourself is not just a way to boost your self-esteem, but the prerequisite to truly loving others. To love yourself is to appreciate your existence in this world. It's about accepting who you are—the good, bad and everything in between. It's about knowing your boundaries and your values and honoring them day in and day out, no matter what the circumstances are. When you have self-love, you teach others how you should be treated by showing them how you treat yourself.

When you love yourself, you're kind to yourself no matter what wrong you do. You're also looking after your mind, body, and spirit and putting yourself first over all things. You know your worth not because of what you look like or what you've achieved, but because loving yourself is your own birthright, no matter what. You can't truly love someone else since you can't give something that you don't have. If you don't love yourself, over time your reserves of life will be exhausted and your relationships will fail and falter because of it. In order to really give love, you need to have it. Only then will you be able to give love unconditionally. Give the love you want to experience to yourself first and you'll find that love in due time.

Self-love is a win-win for everyone. Not only will it provide you with inner happiness, peace of mind, confidence and boost your self-esteem, but it allows you to make healthier and better choices in all areas of your life. You'll be able to truly enjoy others and rejoice in the good fortune of others instead of always wondering why it can't be you because it will be you. The more love you have for yourself, the more it benefits everything and everyone around you.

In a nutshell, self-love is needed before you start loving others. It's the foundation to a healthy romantic relationship. Realize that self-love starts with you being free of any shame, hurt, or anger you have towards yourself. Know that you can't really ever experience true love until you first start loving yourself. Self-love is the greatest love of all, and no other love can beat it.

So what does self-love ultimately look like?

Well, it will differ from person to person. But in essence:

It's about going after your dreams and things that inspire you.

It's about saying no to things and people that don't fit in with your values, beliefs and more.

83

It's about spending time and aligning yourself with people, places and things that motivate and encourage you to be the best version of yourself.

It's about refusing to be swayed by others and owning your own thoughts and opinions.

It's about being kind and gentle with yourself no matter how much you mess up.

It's about having the courage to go out and try new things, explore the world and doing whatever makes you happy.

It's about taking the time to live a healthy life and nourish your mind, body, and soul.

It's about knowing your self-worth and that you are enough.

It's about believing that you are capable of wonderful things and creating the life you've always wanted to live.

It's about choosing to see the good in everything and refusing to let anyone else bring you down.

It's about being positive and letting go of any and all negativity in your life.

It's about being at peace with yourself so that you don't care what anyone else thinks of you.

It's about accepting yourself for all your qualities—the good, bad and ugly.

It's about being happy in your own skin and feeling comfortable with who you are.

Self-love creates great relationships since when you respect and love yourself, you're free from always worrying, thus trusting your decisions and feelings. This, in turn, allows you to be authentic and courageous. You begin to live from the heart and this will lead to becoming a more generous and kinder version of yourself. You'll be able to fight through any self-imposed boundaries to go out and live the life you truly want. This way, you'll become more irresistible when you're comfortable with yourself.

And it's not about wanting and dreaming of the future; it's about enjoying the right now. It's not about loving yourself when you're skinnier or have more money. No, it's about loving yourself in the here and now and deciding that each moment is going to be your best!

Chapter 12
Putting It All Together

*B*reak-ups are tough, especially in a digital age where you can easily see what your ex is doing at any given time of the day. Plus, all the reminders on social media that show what you looked like at your happiest don't help matters, either. After a break-up, you try to pick up the pieces and erase every inch of them out of your lives, but the truth is, you can never completely erase them. They'll be emotional landmines everywhere you turn—on your commute to work, a night out with friends, on your social media accounts—everywhere, which is why it's important that you fully get over someone so that you are strong enough to be able to survive these constant reminders and completely move on.

To be strong, you need to utilize everything you've read in this book and then put them all together. Once you do, you'll be able to face the day without feeling any sorrow or remorse for your break-up and will be able to successfully see a day new with a positive mind and an open heart, ready to take in whatever the day brings.

You'll be able to cross over any emotional landmines with ease and not break down over them or the memories they hold. You'll be at a point in your life where you feel confident about who you are and what you want out of life and your next relationship.

In order to have a real breakthrough, you'll need to recognize the red flags in your past relationship. As much as it may hurt to really analyze your past relationship because of the memories, you'll need to examine what went wrong so that you can look for reoccurring negative patterns or the red flags. This will show you what you need to change when looking for new love in the future so that you can start fresh and not end up in such a negative cycle again.

Figure out why your past relationships have failed to pinpoint a pattern. This way you can recognize what's been going wrong and aim to correct them to make future relationships work. If you don't take the time to recognize these red flags, you'll simply end up making the same relationships mistakes over and over again, stuck in the same pattern that you'll never be able to free yourself from. Each woman has their own red flags, so dig deep and be honest with yourself when trying to pinpoint what went wrong with your exes since it's the only real way to grow. When you choose to ignore the red flags that are obvious to others (and sometimes us), you're only hurting yourself and any true potential of finding true love.

Maybe you chose to stay with someone despite knowing deep down that they weren't the one for you. Or maybe you sabotaged many of your relationships. Whatever it is, be brave enough to locate the mistake and own it. Know that the love you're seeking—the love everyone is searching for—is possible. Everyone can have that happy ending they dream about. For you to get it, you'll have to figure out what's been going wrong in past failed relationships, learn from it so that you don't have the same mistakes and then grow and evolve as a person.

The past is the past. Learn from it and then move on. Don't dwell on it or beat yourself up for it. Whatever your red flags were, recognize that they're your mistakes and then move on from them. Make it a point to actively try not to make them and go into a new relationship fresh. Don't dwell on those mistakes and blame yourself. Leave all baggage in the past so that you can max your potential in that new relationship.

Learning from your past mistakes may be key to moving on, but making yourself a priority is the No. 1 thing you'll need to do after a break-up. In order to have any romantic future with someone, you'll have to make sure that you're in the right state of mind to welcome new love. It's important that you take care of yourself and make your needs and wants a priority.

Take time to find out who you are at this point in your life. You're a totally new person with new insight, and you'll have to get to know who that person is. Spend time with yourself to discover new things that you've never noticed before. Go out and meet new people, take up new hobbies and embrace your new single status. Live it up and be free. You owe it to yourself!

You've just experienced a break-up and need time to build yourself up again.

As you make yourself a priority, you'll develop deeper self-respect and self-acceptance that you never knew you had. And with that, you'll feel more confident in yourself and resilient to go out and find the love that you deserve. To do this, create a no negativity zone by setting boundaries and simply saying no to things that aren't making you happy or serving you. Make it a point to say no to toxic people, unwanted obligations or anything negative that might come into your life when you're in such a vulnerable state. And make sure that you say no if your ex tries to pull you back into another dysfunctional relationship.

Instead, do things that make you happy. Follow your passions and do things that will add value and bliss to your life. Surround yourself with people who will lift you up and support you. Live each day as positive as you can and you'll soon notice that the world around you will also be positive, attracting a person of worth for you.

As you're discovering yourself all over again after a break-up, really take the time to reflect on you and your wants and needs. Don't rush into a new relationship. Wait until you are ready emotionally. Be friends with new guys you meet to see where it can lead. This way, you can get to know them before you do anything rash and end up in the same cycle as before. Remember, you're looking for true love and not Mr. Right now. That could have been one of your red flags, so change the cycle.

Although it might be hard to think that everything will work out for the better while you're in the messy stages of a break-up, you have to have faith that everything will sort itself out. You have to keep positive and know that there is a light at the end of the tunnel although it might look dim at the moment. Every woman who has gone through a break-up has questioned her future and thought no good would come from her break-up; that love will never come to her again. But I promise you things will get better. It may not be tomorrow, or the next day or even next week or next month, but in time, you'll come out of this wondering why you ever had doubts in the first place!

It's time to break-up with self-limiting beliefs.

It's time to break-up with putting everyone else's needs above your own.

It's time to break-up with self-doubt.

It's time to break-up with rejection.

It's time to break-up with negativity.

It's now time for your breakthrough!

Final Note

I hope this book in some way has helped to start you on a path of love and healing.

What are you tolerating in your life? It's time to let go and move on. Whether it's a relationship, friendship, job, etc. Have some self-respect. Free yourself from anything and everything that no longer serves you.

Self-love and confidence changed my life. It allowed me to step outside my comfort zone, embrace my flaws, and be true to who I really am. I want to inspire you to do the same. Pick yourself up and learn to move beyond your circumstances. Make peace with your past and create a new, happier, healthier, more meaningful future. It wasn't until my engagement came to an end that I realized my worth. As I began to learn the principles of self-love and acceptance and implemented them in my life, I experienced a peace unlike any I'd ever known. Now I know it is not only okay, but necessary to speak up for myself, set standards for people I engage with, and live authentically and unapologetically.

Never again will I settle for less than I want and deserve. Life is but a series of relationships. Be grateful for every situation. No matter what happens from a relationship, you will benefit from it. All my past relationship taught me lessons about life and myself. Now that I know better, I'll do better. I'll never forget how at the tender age of 21, a few of my girlfriends and I had made a pact to get married by the age of 25. We were so serious about meeting this deadline. Today, I can only cringe at such a thought. Not only was it ridiculous to set a deadline for something I had absolutely no control of, but 25 is so young. I had barely experienced life. And prior to that, I had only been in one long term serious relationship.

Ladies, singleness is not a death sentence. This is just a chapter in your life. You're not going to be single forever. Use this time to grow and discover who you truly are, so that when you are in a relationship again, you will be the best partner that you can be. Be patient and have faith that love will find you in your own divine timing. There is a season and a time for everything.

What an unbelievable, life transforming, three years it has been. I have overcome what I had thought to be the worst and unapologetically living in my truth. Finding my voice has inspired me to help others find theirs and my life lessons can and will help you conquer self-love in every aspect of your life.

If you take only one thing away from this book, I hope it's this: You are still in process and you still have the opportunity to live the life of your dreams.

I wish you all the best on your personal journey.

Xoxo,

Dalia

About the Author

A dedicated Life Empowerment Coach, Dalia Smith is devoted to encouraging and empowering women who struggle with self-love. Equipped with an M.A in Counseling Psychology and an abundance of experience in the helping professions, she is passionate about coming alongside women to help them build the lasting confidence needed to foster thriving relationships. Overflowing with empathy for those around her, Dalia is committed to inspiring women to grow and achieve and heal, most especially in the areas of romance, love, dating, marriage, and gently moving on from toxic relationships in order to embrace a more vibrant and unbridled future. People, life, and love. These three things are most important to Dalia. And it is her ultimate hope to help others embrace all three with passion, confidence, and authenticity.

Bonus

*B*roken hearted again? I know it hurts. Really bad. Maybe it doesn't feel like it right now, but you CAN heal your heart. Whether you are ready to turn things around, get back up on your feet, dust yourself off and feel good again…or you still want to wallow for a little longer but are ready to start enjoying feeling good about yourself again…I have just the treat for you! These bonus goodies will give you all the tools you'll need to bring back that warm fuzzy feeling of being loved and cared for, having your needs understood, being heard and being appreciated. This time the relationship will be with the most important person in your life—yourself!

This one is a relationship worth investing in. Through all of life's ups and downs, throughout every decade, your relationship with yourself will only ever get stronger. The better you can learn to take care of yourself, the better your life will become, naturally.

You might as well have fun in the process!

No matter how bad it got, there's a way out, and I'm here to help you get there. Indulge in your innermost feelings and transform them into something wonderful. It's time to check out of the Heartbreak Hotel. Treat yourself to a more inspiring destination!

Soul Vows

I vow to comfort myself during times of hopelessness, despair, depression, disillusionment, or any difficulty that arises.

I vow to be my Beloved always and in all ways.

I vow to never settle or abandon myself in romantic partnerships again.

I vow to live in the faith that my life unfolds in mysterious divine perfection.

I vow to honor my spiritual path and create an amazing life whether I am ever legally married or not.

I vow to honor my calling and live my life as a work of art.

Some vows were tender and some fierce—some private, and some to be shared with the world.

Non-Negotiables

What are your deal-breakers?
List them…
1.

2.

3.

4.

5.

6.

7.

8.

9.

10.

Anytime you find yourself compromising your values and beliefs, I want you to look over this list to remind yourself of your non-negotiables. Remember, they are non-negotiables for a reason.

My Self-Care Check-In

Where do I need to take care of myself more?

- This is a quick coaching exercise to help you connect with yourself and find out what you may be needing.

- Simply look at the list below and FIRST score each item out of 10. Then answer "What do I need?"

- Finally answer the quick questions underneath, including ONE action for yourself! NB. It's important that the score is your FIRST response i.e. your initial or gut reaction and how you are actually feeling NOT "shoulds."

- So, let's take a more specific look at what form/s of self-care you might be needing...

Where do I need to take care of MYSELF more?

What do I need? What would raise my score?

How satisfied are you currently in this area?

Score out of 10 (1 is low, 10 is high)

1.

1. My Energy Levels _____/ 10 10_____
2. How Inspired I'm Feeling _____/ 10 10_____
3. Fun and Play _____/ 10 10_____
4. Self-Honesty _____/ 10 10_____
5. Peace and Quiet _____/ 10 10_____
6. Feeling Heard or Seen _____/ 10 10_____
7. Feeling Accepted and Understood _____/ 10 10_____
8. My Friendships _____/ 10 10_____
9. My Physical Appearance _____/ 10 10_____
10. Feeling Loved and Appreciated _____/ 10 10_____
11. My Environment (e.g. home, _____/ 10 10_____
12. Physical Health _____/ 10 10_____
13. My Feelings and Emotional Health _____/ 10 10_____
14. Organization and Simplicity _____/ 10 10_____
15. Being Challenged and Stretched _____/ 10 10_____
16. Learning and Personal Growth _____/ 10 10_____
17. Money/Finances _____/ 10 10_____
18. Connection to Myself _____/ 10 10_____
19. Relaxation and Pampering _____/ 10 10_____
20. Something else: _____/ 10 10_____

What surprised you most about your responses?

What patterns and themes do you notice?

What else do you notice about your responses, that you perhaps haven't mentioned yet?

Finally, write ONE action you will take THIS week to take more care of yourself: